Listen Buddy

HELEN LESTER

 **Harcourt**

Orlando Boston Dallas Chicago San Diego

Visit *The Learning Site!*
www.harcourtschool.com

To Lenesa — Thanks, for listening

This edition is published by special arrangement with
Walter Lorraine Books, an imprint of Houghton Mifflin Company.

Grateful acknowledgment is made to Walter Lorraine Books,
an imprint of Houghton Mifflin Company for permission to reprint
Listen, Buddy by Helen Lester, illustrated by Lynn Munsinger.
Text copyright © 1995 by Helen Lester; illustrations copyright © 1995 by Lynn Munsinger.

Printed in the United States of America

ISBN 0-15-314286-3

1 2 3 4 5 6 7 8 9 10 060 02 01 00 99

Buddy's father had a beautiful big nose.
He was a great sniffer.

Buddy's mother had beautiful big teeth.
She was a great chomper.

Buddy had beautiful big ears.

It didn't matter.

When Buddy's parents sent him to the vegetable
stand to get a basket of squash, he came home with
a basket of wash.

When they asked him to buy fifteen tomatoes, he camc homc with fifty potatoes.

Buddy's father said, "Listen, Buddy, will you please
bring me a pen?"
"Who?" asked Buddy.
"You," said his father.
"Will you please bring me a pen?"
"A what?" asked Buddy.

"A pen," said his father.
"Will you please bring me a pen?"
"Sure," said Buddy.
Buddy's father said, "Listen, Buddy!"

Buddy's mother said, "Listen, Buddy, will you please
get me a slice of bread?"
"Who?" asked Buddy.
"You," said his mother. "Will you please get me
a slice of bread?"
"A what of what?" asked Buddy.

"A slice of bread," said his mother. "Will you please
bring me a slice of bread?"
"Sure," said Buddy.
Buddy's mother said, "Listen, Buddy!"

Somehow Buddy's mind was always wandering too far
away from those beautiful ears.
His parents tried yelling. "LISTEN, BUDDY!"

One day Buddy got permission to go for a long hop.
He had never before been allowed to go beyond
the vegetable stand.
"Listen, Buddy," his parents warned him. "Just remember
that at the end of the road, there are two paths.
The path to the left will lead you around the pond and
back home. But the path to the right will lead you
to the cave of the Scruffy Varmint. And that
Scruffy Varmint has a nasty temper, so be sure to
take the path to the left."
"Right?" asked Buddy.
"Left," said his parents.
"Right!" said Buddy. And with a salute of his paw
he hopped away.

Feeling very grown-up, Buddy hopped along, past the vegetable stand and on to the end of the road.
"Now let's see," he pondered. "Was I supposed to go left or right?"
"Or right?"
"Or left?"

Twenty-five hops later, Buddy discovered that right
was wrong. There in front of his cave was the
Scruffy Varmint, doing scruffy things that varmints do, like
snarling, mussing his hair, rubbing dirt on his knees,
and scratching a whole lot of itches. At his feet
was a large soup pot.
"What are you going to do with that soup pot?"
asked Buddy.
"What does one usually do with a soup pot — bake pie?"
replied the Scruffy Varmint, not too kindly.
"I'm going to make some soup."
"Some what?" asked Buddy.
"Soup," snarled the Scruffy Varmint.

Buddy had forgotten his parents' warning about the
Scruffy Varmint. He asked eagerly, "May I help?"
The Scruffy Varmint was not fond of having company, but
with help he'd have his soup sooner, so he said, "Alllll
right, Bunnyrabbit, come help me gather firewood."
"Who, what?" asked Buddy.
"You. Firewood."
Buddy eagerly hopped ahead of the Scruffy Varmint.
Very gently he gathered a large prickly bundle,
which he held out proudly.

Roughly the Varmint grabbed the bundle. "I said
firewood, not *briarwood*," he yelped, plucking the
sharp thorns from his paws.

Later, when the pot was filled with water, the
Scruffy Varmint lay against a rock, licking his paws
and barking orders.
"Hustle, Bunnyrabbit. Get the flour."
"Yessir!" said Buddy.

"Five pinches of salt."
"Yessir!" said Buddy.
"Fifteen tomatoes."
"Yessir!" said Buddy.

"And a big load of squash."

"Yessir!" said Buddy.

The Scruffy Varmint rose and gave the soup a stir.

He took a taste. It tasted a little like . . . well,

a little . . . maybe it needed some pepper.

"Bunnyrabbit, get the pepper from the left side of the
kitchen sink," the Varmint growled.
"Who get the what from the where side of the where
what?" asked Buddy.

The Scruffy Varmint repeated, "WHO GET THE WHAT FROM THE WHERE SIDE OF THE WHERE WHAT?" Never mind."
He stalked into the kitchen and got the pepper himself and sprinkled it into the soup.
"There," he snarled. "Now, Bunnyrabbit, put the soup on the fire."

Buddy put the soup *in* the fire.

The fire went *Hsssssssssss*.
So did the Scruffy Varmint.
"I'll teach you," he howled. "I WILL have soup!
Bunnyrabbit soup! And I know just the bunny to use,
the Bunnyrabbit who never listens!"
Buddy listened.

He also hopped.
Verryveryvery fast.
Faster than he had ever hopped in his life.

He whizzed up the road past the vegetable stand and
into the safety of his house.

And a little later, when Buddy's parents asked him
to bring a pen and a slice of bread,
Buddy listened.